TREES

By
Robin Twiddy

FOREST EXPLORER

KidHaven PUBLISHING

Published in 2019 by KidHaven Publishing, an Imprint of Greenhaven Publishing, LLC
353 3rd Avenue, Suite 255, New York, NY 10010

This edition is published by arrangement with Booklife Publishing.

Written by: Robin Twiddy
Edited by: Kirsty Holmes
Designed by: Gareth Liddington

Cataloging-in-Publication Data

Names: Twiddy, Robin.
Title: Trees / Robin Twiddy.
Description: New York : KidHaven Publishing, 2019. | Series: Forest explorer | Includes glossary and index.
Identifiers: ISBN 9781534528796 (pbk.) | ISBN 9781534528819 (library bound) | ISBN 9781534528802 (6 pack) | ISBN 9781534528826 (ebook)
Subjects: LCSH: Trees--Juvenile literature. | Forest plants--Juvenile literature. | Forests and forestry--Juvenile literature. | Forest ecology--Juvenile literature.
Classification: LCC QK475.8 T963 2019 | DDC 582.16--dc23

Printed in the United States of America

CPSIA compliance information: Batch #BW19KL: For further information contact Greenhaven Publishing LLC, New York, New York at 1-844-317-7404.

Photocredits: All images are courtesy of Shutterstock.com.

Cover – Fotofermer, hddigital, valzan, EtiAmmos, woe, isak55, violetkaipa, 1 - kpboonjit, 2 - Quick Shot, 3 - Jan Martin Will, 4 - Kiselev Andrey Valerevich, attila, 5 - bogdan ionescu, Dudaeva, Paisit Teeraphatsakool, StudioSmart, 6 - VP Photo Studio, 7 - Bilanol, 8 - Wojciech Piejko, 9 - daizuoxin, LilKar, 10 - Smit, Lizard, ALEXEY GRIGOREV, 11 - Catalin Petolea, 12 - VCoscaron, 13 - paffy, 14 - natthawut ngoensanthia, 15 - Viktor Loki, Burakova_Yulia, 16 - Emaruchi, 17 - Eric Isselee, IrinaK, Richard Peterson, Eric Isselee, 18 - Petr Bonek, 19 - Zhukove Irina, 20 - Christopher Elwell, 21 - michael sheehan, 22 - upsenskaya, 23 - narikan, hofhauser, 24 - NITI JUNKAVEEKOOL.

Images are courtesy of Shutterstock.com. With thanks to Getty Images, Thinkstock Photo and iStockphoto.

CONTENTS

Words that look like **this** can be found in the glossary on page 24.

LET'S EXPLORE

WELCOME, FOREST EXPLORER!

Today we will be exploring the trees of the forest. We will learn about different types of trees, how they grow, and the creatures that live in them.

GRAB YOUR EQUIPMENT

A budding forest explorer will need:

Crayons

Paper

Boots

Notebook

SEE THE FOREST FOR THE TREES

Look around you, forest explorer. What can you see? If the answer is trees, you are probably in the forest. Forests are large areas covered in lots of trees.

Trees can come in all different sizes. Some are really tall with lots of branches. Some are small and leafy. Trees can also be very old.

DECIDUOUS TREES

The leaves change color before they fall off!

Have you ever noticed that some trees lose their leaves in autumn? These are called deciduous trees (say: dee-SID-you-us).

There are lots of different trees that are deciduous, but they all have some things in common. For example, most have **broad leaves.**

Some deciduous trees, like larches, don't have broad leaves.

EVERGREEN TREES

Evergreen trees keep their leaves all year round. Most evergreens are coniferous trees. This means that they have hard leaves called needles or scales.

Most coniferous trees grow in cold areas.

Look at the trees around you. Are they broadleaf or coniferous?

Evergreen trees do lose their leaves. But unlike deciduous trees, they don't lose them all at once and make more all year round.

ALL TREES HAVE...

There are some things that all trees have. All trees have **roots** that grow underground. They also all have a trunk, which is the main body of the tree.

All trees have bark, branches, and leaves. Bark is the outside layer of the tree that acts as the tree's skin.

Are there different trees in your forest? What is different about them?

FRUIT, NUTS, AND SEEDS

Some trees grow fruit such as apples, oranges, and mangoes. Other trees grow nuts. The fruit and nuts contain seeds.

If the seeds find the right soil, they will grow into trees.

When birds and other animals eat the fruit and nuts, they **deposit** the seeds in their poop. This helps the tree spread its seeds farther away.

TREE HOMES

Trees are a good place to find birds.

If you are looking for animals when you are exploring the forest, trees are an excellent place to look. Many animals make trees their homes.

Some other animals you might find living in trees:

Squirrel

Koala

Racoon

Dormouse

Lots of insects and other creepy-crawlies can be found in trees.

TREE SAFETY

Trees can be really fun to play in, but you must be careful. Always make sure that you have an adult explorer with you.

Never climb too high!

If you are going to climb trees, make sure that you have good boots for climbing with good grip.

TREE FUN

You can add your rubbings to your forest explorer's notebook.

Place your paper over the bark of a tree or a leaf. Now rub your crayons over it very hard. You should be able to see the pattern of the bark or leaf on the paper!

What is the biggest tree you can find? Try walking around it, counting your steps until you are back where you started.

Keep a record of how many steps it takes to get around the tree.

KEEPING NOTES

It is really important to keep **accurate** notes. You might not know what types of trees you have seen. Make a drawing of the shape and the leaves so you can look it up later.

You could glue your leaf and bark rubbings in here to help.

How many types of tree did you find in your forest? How many of them can you identify?

GLOSSARY

accurate	precise and careful
broad leaves	flat, wide leaves that are soft and flexible
deposit	to place somewhere
roots	the part of a plant that grows underground and collects water and nutrients from the soil

INDEX